After a Summer Rain

Clifton King

Royale Road Publishing, Carlsbad, California

After a Summer Rain

Copyright ©2020 by Clifton King

All Rights Reserved

First Edition
Text font: Times New Roman
Cover photo and design by author

ISBN: 978-0-9786935-7-2

Library of Congress Control Number: 2020918485

A few of these poems were first published, some in different versions, in *Listen to the Tide* or *Beach Bum*.

Printed in the United States of America

Royale Road Publishing, Carlsbad, California

for family, friends and you

Re-examine all that you have been told.
Dismiss that which insults your soul.
Walt Whitman

Contents:

———————————•———————————

———————————•———————————

━━━━━━━━━━━━━━━●━━━━━━━━━━━━━━━

If the night were poetry,
how would I survive sunrise?

After a Summer Rain

The grass was wet, leaves dripped
that heavenly elixir onto the sidewalk.
Maybe the angels cried or the moon wept
or maybe God looked down and saw
what a mess we have made of his earth
and couldn't contain His sadness.
I remember wiping a tear from my child's
cheek when a tumble or a trip triggered
that emotional outpouring that somehow
makes us feel a little better, maybe even
heals the wound slightly. I don't know
why the streets were wet and the palms
drizzled a small rain storm of their own.
I do know His plan has not played out well.
So, I have cleared a small area behind
the shed that pretends to be my garage,
started construction of an Ark since I don't
envision humankind repenting any time soon.

Indian Beach

A slice of wild Oregon coast,
wide, windswept,
dotted with tide pools.
Sea stacks
rise from the ocean.
We travel the road in,
long and winding,
meandering
beneath a canopy
of coast range forest
thick with evergreens,
carpeted in ferns.
Offshore,
Tillamook Rock Lighthouse
still stands guard
in an oft angry sea.
And in a light summer rain
I kiss her the first time.

Paris Serenade

Outside, skies are dreary with rain.
If only I could write a poem, words
so elegant they would coax the sun
out of hiding, retrieve a speck of summer
to disguise this December day.

On the radio, a jazz station, a clarinet solo
— *Paris Serenade.*

I recall our trip to Paris, our apartment
on rue Paul Albert, that small cafe
at the bottom of the hill where we ate
our first meal, those morning metro rides,
that little bakery around the corner,
wandering the Latin Quarter in search
of Hemmingway's ghost, and those
Paris nights lost in each other's love.

Fires up North

California, Oregon, Washington.
Forests ablaze, light up the night sky, smoke
smothers daylight, the earth unable to breathe.
Flames are the enemy, firefighters our troops.
But the enemy does not die easily, it does not
surrender or retreat until it has consumed
everything, everyone that stands in the path
of its march, its relentless march that some say
will end only when it reaches the sea. *Burn
in Hell,* an expression of anger, a promise made
by the clergy to wrong doers and unbelievers.
But this burn, these all-consuming flames take
the righteous, the innocent, along with the evil.
These are not the eternal flames of Hell,
                              or are they?

Broken Tail Light

for Julian Edward Roosevelt Lewis
a black man
murdered by a Georgia State Trooper
August 7, 2020

The Georgia night,
hot, humid, still as death
along Stoney Pond Road.

Julian Lewis drives alone
through shadowy darkness,
window down, headed home.

Bright lights pierce the night
behind him, blue and red,
brilliant as a shooting star.

A State Trooper approaches.
The racist stench of gunpowder
lingers in the hot Georgia night.

Compassion

He stands on the walkway along Carlsbad's seawall,
beard and hair unkempt, but not frighteningly so,

with that sunburned face of a man who spends
most of his time outside, on the streets, homeless.

Bedroll over his shoulder he leans into the shadow
of lifeguard tower 22. He stares out at the ocean,

maybe thoughts of better days, or maybe just a stare.
There's no way to know his story, what brought him

here, where he came from. But a man fifty feet
down the walk is afraid of what he doesn't know.

He's on his cell phone talking with the police.
He'll probably take a picture, post it on social media,

brag about how he helped clean up the neighborhood.
I continue my walk, wonder when compassion died.

Flea Circus

I watched the RNC the other night.
Actually, that's a lie. But then,
so was the RNC. I saw a flea circus
once, was amazed as a fat man
in need of a bath and haircut
had his fleas jump through hoops,
obey his every command. We,
the uninformed eight-year-olds,
believed every wave of his hand.
As adults we know a flea circus
is an illusion, an act performed
for the gullible, a promise given
with a wink and sinister grin.
That type of deception lives
only in our childhood memories.
                              Or does it?

Normandy on My Mind

We walk the beach south of Cardiff.

A minus tide reveals a stretch of sand
reminiscent of Omaha Beach.

But this beach doesn't have the history
                    or the blood stains.

The Line

The old man swings his sledge.
Again and again the blows echo,
    steel against steel is the song.
Spikes driven deep and fast,
    the rail held strong.
The old man wipes his brow
    and curses the searing heat
    of dark steel in the midday sun.
His body bent from the years
    of steel rails laid one after one.
Sweat glistens on his back.
Only ten more miles on this line,
    ten more miles of hard steel track.

Waiting for Flight 143 to San Jose

Across from us a rotund woman works
on three sweet rolls and a large café mocha.
Her husband lounges in the seat next to her.
His Iowa-white legs protrude from plaid shorts
baggy enough that we know he is a boxers guy.
Electronic devices dominate the waiting area.
Not a book in sight, not a hushed conversation,
just a flurry of thumbs. Thought provoking tweets
and facebook postings: *airport. waiting.*
And, from their equally astute followers, *cool dude.*
I hope the pilot turns off his phone before takeoff.

Book Report:
Under the Tuscan Sun

I read her book again, slowly, sip the words like fine wine,
try to place myself on the page, feel Tuscan soil on my hands
as I bury the tendril of an old grape vine, hope for new growth.
The author speaks of a blue book that becomes this novel. She
talks about her house, the ancient tile roof, iron balcony and
faded green shutters; how when the light changes the house
turns gold, sienna, ocher and spots of scarlet from an old paint
job seep through. And her house has a name. *Bramasole*:
to yearn for the sun. And there I find common ground. I recall
evenings of watching the sun color the sea blood red; listening
to gulls cry in a darkening sky; wishing the horizon would pull
away, let the sun stay. I think of that scribble of words I've
made in notebooks, on random sheets of paper over the last few
decades. The subtext of my poems: yearnings for ocean and sun.
I desperately want to write words, form phrases like this author.
And to that end I have actually stolen a few for this poem.
A crime of passion. I must complete my journey through her
blue book of memories, satisfy a yearning for words, the ocean
and especially the sun.

Wildflowers

Only those who visit the meadow,
pick wildflowers, lie together naked
in a bed of color, wait for petals
to open, unashamed, revealing
the sweet fragrance of passion;
only those who hold the gift
of spring gathered to their body,
whisper, *loves me—loves me not*;
only they know the satisfaction
of love pledged among wildflowers.

The fool doth think he is wise,
but the wise man knows himself to be a fool.
William Shakespeare

Demagoguery

There are flags flying in the afternoon breeze,
across the street, down the block, just as the
Confederate flag was flown for decades
by bigots and racists, by uneducated morons
quick to judge, condemn other human beings.
These new flags carry the name of a man-child
who praises white supremacists, locks children
in cages, denies health care to millions,
refuses to believe the scientific community,
dismisses global warming because it still snows,
claims the COVID-19 pandemic is a hoax,
never expresses grief for the thousands dead
from his inaction, his fear of bad numbers;
a man-child who makes fun of the physically
impaired, openly insults women and minorities,
curries favor from dictators and tyrants,
claims genius status, yet can't piece together
a complete sentence, can't live without
the adulation of his pathetically ignorant faithful;
a man-child who is not interested in anything
other than how much he can profit
while denying many the basic dignities of life.
These flags flap like a mental deficient shouting
I am the king, I am the king, I am the king.
No one believes it but him.
Wave that flag you fool.
The Emperor has no new clothes.

Evening Lights

The sun has fallen from the sky,
slipped behind a bank of fog
that sticks to the horizon
like frosting on a cake.
But the sky is still bright with
leftover light, an apricot glow
shattered here and there by
palm silhouettes. A half moon
creeps across the westerly sky
waiting to dominate the night,
unashamed to out shine any star.
Across the street, the blue flashes
of a television lights up a window.
Above me, the porch light flickers on.
Darkness marches in from the east
as the leftover light rushes off
to be near the now invisible sun.

Apple Fire 2020

Life is unfair but remember
sometimes it is unfair in your favor.
— Peter Ustinov

A gray fold of fog lies
along the California coast.
Morning sun pushes night away.
A breath of breeze rattles
palm fronds, carries a lazy line
of pelicans in wingless flight.

But inland, on desert's edge,
an inferno gnaws at the earth,
swallows scrub pine—everything.
Curls of smoke fill the sky.
Wildlife scurries in panic.
People abandon their dreams.

Stolen Afternoon

I catch a glimpse of her
in a sidewalk café,
then later, down by the sea.

She strolls the sandy shore
barefoot, sun on her face.

I follow her footprints,
catch her eye, ask her name.

She tells me the afternoon
is ours and that is when
the rest of my life begins.

Barely There
after the photo art of Monica Royal

I'd like to shed a little more
light on this not-so-subtle
suggestion of a woman, delve
deeper into the details. Yet,
I will say there is not a curve
out of place. And that drape
of fingers over hip, the angle
of her elbow—mesmerizing.
But, it's really about the artist's
struggle with light and shadow
like a poet agonizes over words
—and what to leave unsaid.

Home

I can't recall
the first time
I gave myself
to the Pacific Ocean,
cold swirl of sea
around me,
a baptism,
an acceptance
of its healing powers,
my giving over
of spirit and soul,
the sea's
unspoken promise
to always be there.
It seems
I have never been
anywhere else
except this place,
this home of my being.

Love Letters

Someday, when family gathers to say goodbye,
when we are mere memories on this earth,
when they sort through what we left behind,
there will be no shoebox of love letters
hidden away beneath winter coats and scarfs
or in the dark recesses of a dresser drawer;
no words from another, in another time,
stationary saturated with someone's soul,
words that should never be unearthed,
displayed like the bones of an Egyptian King.

I remember writing love letters to a girl
whose crystal blue eyes said, kiss me.
I remember the letters she sent, scented
with body powder that made my heart race
before I read a single word. I miss
love letters put to paper with pen in hand.
I miss the swirl of a capital *G*, the stiff
back of an *I* and the finality of the mailbox.

Now, notes, poems and love letters travel
between cell towers and appear on a screen
to be read, maybe reread, then deleted.
But remember this my friend, a deleted
email does not diminish our friendship.

Renga

blue butterfly wings
dancing on a prairie wind
midst orange milkweed

gentle snows bury the seeds
sleeping blossoms await spring

dolphins sapphire flight
pirouette and slip beneath
and we can only wish

pelican wings paint the sky
glorious motion colors

morning glories twine
blaring trumpets rejoicing
blue and lavender

crows cry in the morning sky
black in the brilliant blue air

Alpha & Omega

The gray mist of morning clings to the palms.
Seagulls roost on the sand near water's edge.
I walk barefoot in the cool shallows of the Pacific.

This is where I was born, birthed by mother ocean,
salt water in my veins, swaddled in seaweed.
I need salt air, a fresh ocean breeze to fill my lungs;

a constant surge of sea, that pulse of creation.
I need the sun, its life-giving warmth on my body;
that mystical mosaic of shells on beach sand.

This is where I began, where I want to end.

Artist

Light and shadow,
the artist's love.

Oh, to be
an instant of sunlight,
a fleeting shadow.

If I Could Choose the Day I Die

I don't want to die on a cloudy day,
sun hidden behind a cumulus face,
a great gathering of grays,
a day when the sky is about to cry.

I don't want to die on a cloudy day,
a day when that meandering flight
of pelicans is nearly invisible
in the monochromatic heavens.

I want to die on a sunny day
when the sky is a blistering blue
and the sea can't decide whether
to celebrate my life, or weep.

I want to die on a sunny day
when palm shadows streak
the sidewalk and I can see
my final sunset in your eyes.

I want to die on a sunny day
so after we kiss goodbye
you can go out to your garden,
tend the flowers and miss me.

A Woman's Smile

When I was sixty-eight it was a very good year.
In a garden of youthful wishes I risked it all
for a woman I desperately wanted.......to know.

It's cliché to say her beauty took my breath away,
yet, it did. And that dinner invitation, a scripted move.
But what's a man to do when he sees his future
                              in a woman's smile?

Poets utter great and wise things
which they do not themselves understand.
                                    Plato

First Beach Walk in Two Months
May 4, 2020

This morning the sun shines
a brilliant white in a pale
eastern sky. Yet, fog huddles
against the coastline,
a damp curtain over the sea.
An undecipherable prophecy.
I fill a thermos with coffee,
a survival kit of sorts, head
for the beach. Fletcher Cove.
The parking lot closed,
taped off like a crime scene.
But foot traffic is allowed,
exercise only, don't stop,
don't stand around, wear a mask.
What the sign really means is:
Don't let COVID-19 catch you.
Think of how safe life would be
on the Serengeti if the zebra,
water buffalo and gazelle
were given such a warning.
Don't stop. Don't stand around.
Think of the lioness' frustration,
the hunger in her pride's belly.
I pull on my mask, check
over my shoulder for that nasty
COVID-19 and start down the beach.
A red tide laps at the sand.
The surf is small, inconsistent,
yet a few of the foolish venture
into the algae soup. A stink
hangs in the air, replacing
the early morning fog.
And it looks as if everyone
just pulled off a bank robbery.
But—what a glorious walk.

Survival

A small pittosporum forest grows alongside our house, rangy, untamed, home to a tortoise named Maize. Relentlessly she roams in search of food and probably a male tortoise. She snaps at the orange soles of my running shoes, crawls across my feet, continues her search. I'm reminded of days in the distant past, me, waist deep in some Oregon river, flow meter clicking away, recording a moment in time. In that river, salmon on their upstream quest to spawn, swim between my legs, unafraid, drawn by something as powerful as the love that pulls one person to another. I'm reminded that survival is the primary pursuit in the animal kingdom. But humans have other concerns, often take survival for granted. Sure, the sun will rise again tomorrow, our next heart beat unchallenged. Unless—you are that woman living in her car with two small children; the man who lost his job nine months ago, unemployment benefits running dry; or the five-year-old boy and his four-year-old sister from south of the border living in a cage for months, parents detained elsewhere. True, survival is not a given. Yet, it is not something that should be denied because of a broken society.

Dog Owner's Response
to the *Idiot Elect's* Face Mask

He is wearing a face mask, finally.
His mouth is covered, finally.
His words are mumbled, as usual.
We cannot hear his racism,
    hatred and outright lies, thankfully.
If only that black face mask
    were a black bag over his head.
Then we could dispose of it
    like a bag of dog shit.

Alone

I sit alone wondering when
the world will return
to normal, whatever that is.
I haven't been in the ocean
for what seems a lifetime,
nor been to the corner cafe
for coffee with friends,
haven't seen my granddaughter
since COVID-19 came to town.

Then a small light appears,
(not to be cliché, but maybe like
that light at the end of a tunnel)
in the form of a friend's poem.
Now, I can't wait for dusk,
the curtain lifted on that dance
of stars, the cool embrace
of the moon's second-hand light.
And so, with this gift
of her words I no longer feel
like that lone cypress in Monterey.

Last Kiss

Saint Mary's Hospital, stark and angular,
rises from a clutch of medical buildings.
I dread that trek through the maze of corridors
that leads to Mother's room, the clutter of apparatus,
tangle of tubes and wires. She is lost in a rumple
of covers and pillows, confined by padded bed rails.
She smiles. In that moment, for that moment, my fears
vanish. She speaks so softly I barely hear her words,
lean down close to her face. She kisses my cheek.
                                        Her last kiss.

A Morning with Father

He sits across the room from her
even though she is gone.
Coffee steams in his cup,
cream, no sugar. One cup
in the morning—alone.
I talk to her every day, he says.
Then, memories fill the silence.
Memories of before. Pieces
of life scattered across
the country, around the world.
Providence, Rhode Island;
Pratt, Kansas; Pearl Harbor;
San Carlos, Mexico;
Belmopan, Belize;
Long Beach, California;
San Jose, Costa Rica.
They don't last long you know,
the men left behind,
the women seem to do better.
It's been nearly a year.
You'd never know she is gone.
Nothing in the house has changed
except—the look in his eyes.

Trust Fund Babies

What was it Jeff called them?
Oh yes, trust fund babies.
Middle-aged men gathered around
a beach bench at La Jolla Shores.
Middle-aged men joking and laughing
that same inane babble spewed out
by immature teenagers.
Mid-aged men who should
be at work on a Tuesday at 11AM.
But trust fund babies don't work,
never have worked and don't want
to work. Life's a free ride.
There's a constant flurry of high-fives,
and "Dude" echoes off the sidewalk
like storm surf. Well, it is a surf culture
of sorts: they congregate at the beach.
I suppose if it were the 40's you'd hear
"hep cat" and "give me some skin".
Trust fund babies just want to belong,
to be somebody. Yet we all know
you can't be somebody by sitting
on your ass all day, every day.

Since the Beginning

I've been thinking about you.

Not only since that first time
I glimpsed your face shaded
by that floppy sunhat, saw
your smile, heard you laugh.

I've been thinking about you
since the beginning of time.

New Year's Day 2019
a few days after my 75th birthday

Morning air bites at my face.
Beach cobbles rattle
with every attack of waves
that rolls ashore.
The sky is pale blue,
nearly white along the horizon
where the early sun
paints the sea silver.
I walk water's edge,
sand cool, damp
beneath bare feet.
This is the way to begin
a new year. This is the way
it should end someday:
the memory of me, the sea
and an ocean breeze.
And when the current is right
I'll drift north, join my father
when he returns on the tide.

Early Morning Encounter
with Two tRump Trolls

The early sky is gray with scant clouds,
our dogs eager for their morning walk.
On the street, a couple walk side by side.
I greet them with a *good morning*.
They glance our way, then, at the sign
in our front window: *Biden for President*.
There is no response, there is no nod,
no desire to speak to Biden's people.
And then I notice it, a slight goose step.
Is that one of Hitler's platoons, maybe
a Mussolini marching band, though
I don't see any instruments, only
the dazed look of the brainwashed,
the mindless sheep who follow
the snake oil salesman, the con artist,
the wanna be, oh so wanna be emperor.
They march on without a word,
without a mask, without a clue.

Ensenada Cruise

Ensenada, squalid city
of barren brown hills
littered with small shacks,
apartment buildings
the color of gum drops.

Downtown, street vendors
hawk trinkets, swarm tourists
like lepers begging for alms,
and brown faced children stare
with innocent eyes of hunger.

Lover

She is here, waiting, where I last left her.
I touch her, she me, for the first time in months.
We have been together for a lifetime—my lifetime.
She was there in the beginning:
And the Spirit of God was hovering over the face of the waters.
Her names are as many as the stars.
Yet, I have only known her as the Pacific.
This name, from the Latin *pacificus.* Peaceful.
She welcomes me back, doesn't ask where I have been
as I immerse myself in her peaceful liquid embrace.

Poetry is an echo, asking a shadow to dance.
                    Carl Sandburg

Fall

Leaves do not turn and fall
here along the California coast
like in New England. We don't
have to rake that kaleidoscope
of demise into small mounds
for ceremonial disposal later.

Our highways are not littered
with yellow and orange that
take flight with every passing car.
We don't have those skeletal
silhouettes scratching the belly
of gray winter skies.

But, once you stand on a beach,
ankle deep in the ocean, watch
the sun kiss a waiting horizon
then drown itself in the sea,
you will know the beauty
of a New England fall
            is not God's best work.

The New Litter

We cross Avenida Encinas, time our dash
between morning commuter traffic.
Our dogs pull on their leashes, eager to get
to the grass, eager to do their dog thing.
A power mower roars above traffic noise,
spits green remnants onto the sidewalk.
A runaway sprinkler fills the gutter
with reclaimed water. Signs caution us:
No Tome El Agua. We carry bags to pick up
our dog's litter. But lately a new litter
has surfaced: used face masks, in the gutter,
on the sidewalk, tossed into the shrubbery.
When we have no further use for something,
we humans simply toss it. We have found
yet another way to disrespect Mother Earth.

Beachcombing Bounty
for Katie Rose

I save you a slice of summer sun,
a few grains of beach sand,
pack it all away in a shell
I find half buried by the sea,
the blood of high tide still shiny
on those ringed ridges of its back.
There is a necklace of kelp
tangled and knotted along shore.
But you are not one for jewelry.
So, I leave it for the incoming tide
or those children chasing seagulls.
I gift you my beachcombing bounty
as if it holds some value.
Your smile confirms what I knew
from the beginning:
the sea, with her unpredictable sky,
is no longer my first love.

Morning Moon

A small plane overhead
disturbs my morning coffee.

I lift my eyes from the poem
I'm working on, glance up.

At that moment
a Monarch butterfly flits into sight.

Her flight, a dance. Her partner,
an early morning sea breeze.

And beyond both, slowly sinking
in a slate blue sky, the moon.

Nothing Else to Give

I offer this poem
because I have nothing else to give.
Come inside, hide from that cold
wind that wends its way
down the California coast.
Let this poem be a blanket of warmth.
Wrap yourself in these words.

These images are all I have to offer:
long purple shadows of Saguaros
birthed by a red desert sunset,
cactus wren quiet for the night,
sky ablaze with heaven's spectacle.

Please accept my offer of these words:
a cold mountain stream, cutthroat
hiding in the shadows of the shallows,
water too cold for skinny dipping,
yet the bank thick with pine needles
where we can spread our blanket,
fall in love all over again.

I offer this poem
because I have nothing else to give.
So let go of today, come with me
into these words. Allow images
to wash over you, let the silence
between these lines comfort you.

January 20, 2020
surfer's lament

The morning sea is stormy
with whitecaps and chop,
cold as an Arctic flow.
A gray streaked sky
presses down, holds
this frigid January air captive.

A slant of sunlight forces
through a distant break,
lays a luminous silver swath
across the ocean with only
an illusion of warmth.
There is little reason to paddle out,
every reason to just be here.

Wavelengths

Blue is the desert sky after a summer rain,
a mountain lake in the late afternoon.

Gold, a Kansas prairie on a summer day,
the lingering clouds under a September moon.

Red is the sunrise on a cold, clear morning,
the flight of a hawk on wing overhead.

Yellow, a cloudless sunset over the Pacific,
a field of sunflowers in the spring.

Silver is the moonlight on fresh snow,
the wake of a boat under sail.

White, a wave spent, dying on a rocky shore,
the far-away spout of a Humpback whale.

Green is a dolphin's playful leap from the sea,
a barrel cactus jutting into the Arizona sky.

Black is the long shadow of night,
death, eternity, the absence of light.

Sestina for Father

This would have been his 92nd year,
a celebration of all that makes a life:
his roots in a Kansas farm family,
the miles he walked to school each day,
riding the rails to nowhere, any train,
then the CCC and on to the service.

Nearly a decade passed in the service
of his country, the war lingered year
upon year, and the men he trained
as gunners fell, lost their lives
and he knew it would be, until the day
of surrender, that day his family

would welcome his return, and all families
could pretend to forget what their service
had done to these men, today, yesterday,
beyond the horror of those years.
It was a time of new beginnings, a new life,
a return to school, a new job, to train

for the future, or sadly for some, hop a train
to the past, leaving friends and family
to wonder about their values of life,
that dedication. Was it just lip service
like so many resolutions on New Year's,
trying to erase mistakes made every day?

But my father rose above that, the day
he came home to California, a short train
ride where he had time to plan for the years
ahead, riches of this new world for his family,
a house in the suburbs, new dishes, a service
for eight for his new wife, for this new life.

Yet, it wasn't only the wealth of fresh life
he wished for, it was more like every day
filled with the joy you find in a church service,
that soul shattering sense of love a train
wreck couldn't loosen, that bond of family
members that lasts far beyond the years.

Yes, this is his 92nd year, and he spent every day
in the service of his beloved wife and family:
a long train ride from farm boy to giver of life.

Seaside Healing

I sit in the shade
of a gnarled coastal pine
this summer look-alike
November day.

A line of pelicans
stitches clouds to sky
above sea scarred
bluffs of Del Mar.

The bite of rotting kelp,
sweetness of sunscreen,
and ocean mist memories
fill the emptiness you left.

Looking for Answers in the Night Sky

The night air is heavy, unbreathable,
as if the door to Hell has been left ajar.
The air conditioner labors in the window
spewing cool air like a minister's oration
on forgiveness and the kingdom of heaven.
Unable to sleep I wander outside, think
I might see the face of God in the night sky,
ask Him about the heat, wildfires up north,
dual hurricanes in the Gulf, the *Derecho*
that leveled ten million acres of crops,
this world-wide pandemic, thousands dead.
I peer into a sparsely starred night, a sliver
of new moon already low in the western sky,
wonder if the good times are really over.
Listen. Is that thunder I hear, or hoofbeats
of the Four Horsemen of the Apocalypse?

A Fool's Flag
in disrespect of #45

The fool down the street
has a new flag flying.
It makes a statement
he is unable to see,
understand: Loser.
Even the curling wind
won't allow it
to remain unfurled.
The fool's flag struggles
to rise to the occasion
while twisted around
its own staff, unable
to display its ridiculous
propaganda. The flag,
like the moron's name
emblazoned on it,
pathetically inept.
The wind is my friend.

Poetry is eternal graffiti written in the heart of everyone.
Lawrence Ferlinghetti

I Watch My Wife in Her Garden

I watch as she digs in the rich loamy soil.
Bare hands fondle delicate roots, press
them into where they will thrive, bloom,
seed themselves into returning next season.
Then that precise process of deadheading,
removing spent blossoms with a twist,
a nip between fingertips. She talks softly
to the flowers, speaks sharply to weeds,
stops to watch a lizard scurry across
the brick planter and disappear behind
a small rose bush in full flower. Yet,
after watching her for an hour in the garden,
what I find simply spellbinding is the sunlight
in her hair and that smile on her face.

Father's Yard

the skeleton of a mulberry
                     stands watch
bird feeders & odd ornaments
dangle from its branches

fractured shadows
spill across the gravel
creep toward the porch

doves and finches search
bobbing & pecking
rejoicing with the discovery
                     of each seed

Father watches from the porch
but sees only the past
Mother's chair empty
                     for a year now

One With the Pacific

After recent high tides and strong surf
the California coast is a ribbon of cobble
embankments that rattles as each wave
clamors ashore. I do the *rock dance*
across cobbles down to water's edge.
The Pacific pulses around me, water
cool, but not as cold as the Atlantic
that day I waded in at Omaha Beach.
I stand at the edge of the earth.
Every wave that washes over my feet
sucks sand back out to sea. Soon
I am buried ankle deep, entrenched,
rooted in the sea like a California kelp.
Once again, I am one with the Pacific.

Masks Required

The July sky is gray with uncertainty.
A lazy line of cars creeps up the coast
in typical summer fashion. Beachgoers
wander the edge of the highway, wait
for a chance to dash toward the beach,
claim a small piece of sandy real estate.
From my van radio Merle Haggard
poses the question: *Are the good times
really over for good?* I have an answer,
but keep it to myself. Traffic inches
into downtown Carlsbad, sidewalks
crawling with swarms of tourists.
Everywhere, signs proclaim: Masks Required.
It's the best thing we can do for each other,
the easiest way to combat the COVID creature.
It's a show of respect for our fellow humans.
Yet, the glare from bare faces in the sun
is nearly as frightening as that blinding
flash of light that births a mushroom cloud.

Passing Through

The morning sea, smooth as a child's face.
Not a breath from the sky, only that sigh
of our ship slipping between Cabo
and that unfathomable point
                     where sea and sky converge.
Our last glimpse of Baja,
mother watching over the bounty of her womb,
barren bronze peninsula cradles the Sea of Cortez
where whales breed and birth in her depths,
dolphins and seabirds free
                     as the day of creation.
We sail past, strangers in that realm.
Then the solemn silhouette of a tanker appears,
a far-off scar on a fresh horizon. A sad song
rises from the sea, the memory of an errant Captain,
a pristine shore. And we are reminded,
                     the array of God's creatures finite.
Yet, it seems there is always one more tanker.

Boy Chasing Birds

A boy chases gulls down the beach.
His stride ungainly, spindly legs
like a young colt. He tosses cobbles
harvested from wet sand exposed
by a minus tide. His arm, his aim
hold no promise of an MLB career.
His father shouts, *Don't throw rocks.*
Seagulls light farther down the beach,
perhaps expecting compliance.
But the boy gathers more cobbles.
And soon, gulls take flight.

Cacophony

Oh, to return, back those many years
to the comfort and quiet of the womb.
The only sound, muted echoes
of my tiny fetus heart.
How was I to know what lurked outside,
what vile intrusions awaited?
The obscene voice of the world:
the senseless chatter and laughter
outside a hotel room door;
the roar of a jet streaking overhead;
that inane babble of cell phone junkies;
car alarms chirping and bellowing
and screaming in the night;
the obscenity, the insult of Rap;
leaf blowers whining;
power mowers humming;
the invasion of a sales-pitch phone call;
the clatter and slap of idiot skateboarders;
the hiss of air brakes;
the muffled cry of a transit bus;
the un-muffled rumble of a Harley;
the squeal of a loose fan belt;
screech of worn brakes;
a blaring public address system;
the prolonged scream of a train whistle;
that cry of a spoiled child;
the clatter and clink
of dishes in a restaurant kitchen;
the ringing and ruckus of a train crossing;
the wail of a police siren
and perpetual barking of a neighbor's dog.

How I long for a symphony of silence.

Desert Marigolds
on the old Oregon Trail

How cruel those distant blue mountains
must have seemed as they edged closer
for weeks as you tramped this desolate desert.
A ghost of that forgotten road snakes west,
etched into this unforgiving soil by ox drawn
wagons and settlers who walked across
the continent chasing a dream, a better life.
That yellow patch of desert marigolds
on the right, just before that rise
where the road bends north, is where
a wagon stopped and Claire McDougall
gave birth to her seventh child, Collin.
They buried Claire there on the edge
of the desert in the same earth that would
become the McDougall homestead.
This road has been forgotten by most.
Yet, those blue mountains, seemingly
as distant as the winter moon that lights
this sage and scrub brush, remember
the life that ended, the life that began
alongside this dusty desert passage
in that patch of desert marigolds.

Mid-Morning at Ponto Beach

I went beachcombing today.
The sea restless, somewhat upset by a far-off storm.

A torrent of water rushed between Ponto jetties
as low tide tried to empty Batiquitos Lagoon.

Broken shells littered the shore,
sand still dark, damp from yesterday's rain.

Two women wandered water's edge, inspecting cobbles
before dropping them into shopping bags.

A young girl walked her dog down to the water,
turned it loose to chase seagulls.

I looked for a heart shaped cobble or a piece of driftwood
to bring home to you, but found only those bits
of broken shells I mentioned.

But you know the best thing about beachcombing?
After I have filled my lungs with sea air,
listened to a hundred waves break, felt the sun on my face,
I get to come home to you.

Baja Ride
Circa 1972 riding a BSA 500cc single

Yesterday the road from Ensenada to San Felipe
was nothing more than a dry, meandering scar
across the Baja peninsula. We raised a dust cloud
that didn't settle until nightfall. But this morning,
rain ricochets off the Sea of Cortez. The musty odor
of wet earth hangs heavy in the air. We eat a breakfast
of eggs, beans and warm tortillas in a small cantina
packed with locals. A din of rapid-fire Spanish fills
the room. A blue haze of cigarette smoke smothers us.
Unable to postpone our departure any longer
we head west toward the Pacific and Highway One.
Rain pelts our helmets and goggles, stings our faces.
When we reach Diablo Dry Lake the rain stops,
the sky begins to clear. Baja resembles a moonscape:
ragged ravines, plateaus, faint purple of distant mountains.
The small town of Colonia Cardenas lies in a narrow valley
just beyond the Sierra De Juarez mountain range.
We find the local bar. No glass in the windows, no door
in the doorway. Inside, more shadow than light. The beer
is cool, not cold. We eat tortillas filled with a cheese-like
substance, leafy greens, possibly lettuce, and a killer salsa
made from jalapeños and nitroglycerin. Once home
it takes two days for the numbness to leave your back side,
a week before your sinuses are free of Baja dust. And never
again will you believe Taco Bell is really Mexican food.

Crows in the Fountain

Evenings I sit and listen
to the music of water on water,
that soft splatter of our fountain
floods the porch. But,
morning brings the crows.
They frolic in the fountain,
fight among themselves
for the best perch. The flap
of wings, snap of beaks,
the constant commotion
dislodges the fountain head.
It falls toward the edge,
shoots water into the garden.
The crows leave, fountain dry,
pump desperately sucking air.
But, I can't get angry.
Crows aren't there for
the song of water on water
and I don't want to play in it.
Yet, we all enjoy the fountain.
A message from the universe.
We should heed her words.

COVID Clouds

When I was a child, my mother
and I would lie on the backyard
lawn and watch clouds. Our dog
didn't understand why we were
on the ground, in his territory.
He licked our faces and barked.
Mother always found animals
in the clouds. I saw only sky,
the motion of clouds, slow
and deliberate. Often, I watched
the sun disappear, reappear
and sometimes slip so low
toward the horizon I didn't
see it again until morning.
Today, sixty days into this
COVID-19 shelter-in-place ordeal,
more than half a century since
Mother and I cloud watched,
I drink tea on the porch, dogs
at my feet, sun sinking low
and I see a skull in the clouds.

Only the very weak-minded refuse
to be influenced by literature and poetry.
                                Cassandra Clare

Doubt

When that gray cloud of doubt
hovers above my horizon
I recall our first kiss;
that crescent moon suspended
in a sky scant with stars;
night air, cool as the Pacific
itself, caressing our faces;
the way our bodies
reached out for each other;
and that runaway train
that was my heartbeat.

When doubt comes around
I recall the time we cried together
when someone sang
How Great Thou Art;
how you brought chicken soup
when I was ill (or was that
just a ruse to see you again?)

When doubt sneaks in
I recall your compassion
for all people, good & not so;
how you tolerate
my black & white opinions
and how we still want each other
after the skirmishes.

Finding an Old Vase in the Attic

Peering into the shadows
of your mouth
it's as if, like a full moon,
you have swallowed the night.

In my hand, fingers conform
to your curves like a suckling child
at her mother's milk laden breast.

I lift you to my ear, wonder
if you hide something
the way a sea shell
holds the ocean prisoner.

I inhale your emptiness.
spring comes to mind, a sea
of Green Parrot Tulips.

And I remember the cut flowers
you cradled every Sunday morning.
Flowers Father gave to Mother.

In Search of Steelhead

When wading a small stream in search of steelhead
time is something better left behind,
your mind a leaf adrift on cool waters
surrendering to tree and meadow grass.

Time is something better left behind
when you are alone in the woods
surrendering to tree and meadow grass
that rod n' reel ritual at water's edge.

When you are alone in the woods
sword ferns and knotted roots confirm
that rod n' reel ritual at water's edge
as sun slips across the sky. Long shadows lie

where sword ferns and knotted roots confirm
steelhead holding in soft shade of the shallows
as sun slips across the sky. Long shadows lie
just below the surface of rippled sunlight.

Steelhead holding in soft shade of the shallows,
that hypnotic flash of silver rainbows
just below the surface of rippled sunlight
gives hope that God has heard your prayers.

That hypnotic flash of silver rainbows,
your mind a leaf adrift on cool waters
gives hope that God has heard your prayers
when wading a small stream in search of steelhead.

Waiting Out COVID-19

I was the summer sun, you the horizon.
You waited under a purple sky
for my evening kiss the way lovers wait
for a moment alone to say, *I love you*.
I was a factory worker waiting to punch
the timeclock while clean-handed office
staff waited their turn at the coffee machine.
Long ago, we were school children waiting
on Mother for a ride home, not unlike
a surfer waiting for a smooth-faced wave.
Once we were a couple dining out, waiting
on our waiter like bees wait for spring flowers.
We were all these and more before. Today,
I am merely a poet waiting on my muse,
waiting for words, like a rodeo cowboy
waits for that first leap of a bucking bronc.

The Girl in San Felipe

I was a young man when we met.
Her skin, brown from the Mexican sun;
eyes, dark as our morning coffee.
Her father was a fisherman,
the Sea of Cortez his domain.
He didn't think much of a Gringo
courting his daughter. I told him
of my intentions, explained
that I loved her, and she me.
His dislike turned to hostility.
But I was a young man, foolish
perhaps, and his bitterness
didn't dampen my bravado.
Then, I met her four uncles.
Nothing was lost in translation.
El Familia is strong south
of the border. I was a young man
when I said good-bye to Maria.
I was a young man who wanted
to someday be an old man.

Blue Wedding Dress

The wedding date set, the bride orders a dress.
It is a traditional white. A white you might find
on the peak of Everest, a clean, sparkling white.

The dress arrives….blue. Blue as a cloudless
desert sky. She sends it back, orders another.
It arrives two days before the wedding…..blue.

Where to place the blame:
that ten-year-old girl, laboring in a sweat shop,
sewing seams, hemming and attaching lace;
the poor woman in shipping, working two jobs
to support three children, one barely off her breast?

Nothing can be done. The universe has spoken.
The bride is beautiful in a blue wedding dress.
But that woman in shipping still has
ten hours before the end of her shift;
that child laborer has nothing in her future.

Sunsets in Sedona

A river, made of memories
of you and me, flows turbulent
through my mind most nights.
I try to sleep on the same sheets
where we once loved and laughed,
where so much of our future was
written with finger tips and lips.
Those desert days are gone,
buried in a dust that choked
every long-neglected promise:
our little house in Sedona;
that deck I built one summer;
a pledge to watch sunsets together.
I'm not sure when the change
came about, when that clear sky
surrendered to foreboding clouds,
when you stopped loving me.

Couple on a Bench

She leans into him, full length of her body
presses against his with the intent of intimacy.
Her left hand drapes across his arm, fingers
slightly curled, not holding, just touching.
Her red dress flows with enticement,
like the flurry of a Matador's cape.
Legs revealed, crossed at the knees,
slant into him. The length of his arm rests
against her breast, long bone of her thigh.
His clothing banal. His relaxed slouch
exudes confidence, or indifference.
Her wide white hat worthy of a poem all its own.

In the Morning

The scent of lovemaking lingers
and my mouth remembers
that you taste like the sun.

Then, I find your damp towel
in my shower, one earring
under the coffee table.

A note on the kitchen table
reads: *I Love You.*
I can't catch my breath.

Leaf Blower:
The lazy man's broom
and an affront to the environment.

He owns an old truck, some dull
hedge trimmers and a leaf blower.
He's a landscaper, a gardener,
a man with little or no knowledge
of horticulture, the seasonal play
of buds, blooms, plant dormancy.
His favorite tool, the leaf blower.
An instrument of environmental
destruction: noise pollution worse
than any heavy metal band, screams
of those toddlers across the street,
that freight train that rolls though
every Thursday around midnight.
The small gas engine spews oily
exhaust into the air, coats the earth
with petro-slim. Billows of dust
float through the neighborhood,
no need for a broom or dustpan.
He loads his environment killing
tool and rushes off before his
deadly deed is seen for what it is,
before he can be brought before
The ICC, prosecuted for crimes
against humanity, stripped of his
license to rape the environment.

(Written while trying to enjoy morning coffee on my porch.)

COVID-19 Hair

My hair hasn't been this long since 1961
when we first danced at the Rendezvous Ballroom
on Balboa peninsula. Dick Dale and the Del-Tones.
The *Surfer's Stomp*. My hair, shoulder length, white
from summer sun and salt water; a perpetual peeling
sunburned nose. Everything that shouted *surf dude*
before *dude* was a part of the surf community vernacular.
You, the quintessential *California Girl* The Beach Boys
sang about: young and lithe, a sun goddess tan,
sun-bleached locks that fell freely down your back,
flew untamed in the gentlest sea breeze. But I recall
long hair was also a statement, an in-your-face aimed
at anyone who represented *The Establishment*, whatever
that meant. And then, there was the Broadway hit *Hair*
where everyone on stage got naked. Not sure what
that had to do with hair, but it sold a lot of tickets.
My hair is COVID-19 shelter-in-place long, 1961 long,
over my collar, over my ears, falling in my face long.
Strangely, I have this desire to dance and go surfing.
And, I have this overwhelming urge to get naked.

If my poetry aims to achieve anything, it's to deliver people from the limited ways in which they see and feel.

Jim Morrison

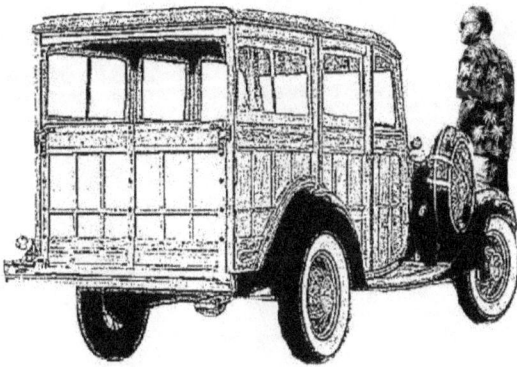

Royale Road Publishing, Carlsbad, California

www.ingramcontent.com/pod-product-compliance
Lightning Source LLC
Chambersburg PA
CBHW051734040426
42447CB00008B/1125